A souvenir guide

Carlyle's House

London

National Trust

The Carlyles

'Carlyle and his wife were a most original and entrancing pair, and their Chelsea history is as fascinating as a fairy tale!'

Henry James

Below **Thomas Carlyle;** pencil-and-wash drawing by Samuel Laurence, 1838

Thomas Carlyle (1795–1881)

Today, Carlyle is not a fashionable figure, but in the 1830s and '40s he was an immensely influential social commentator and historian who shaped the way the Victorians thought about themselves. Among those he influenced were Charles Dickens, William Morris and Octavia Hill, one of the founders of the National Trust. His ideas were also much discussed in the United States and across the English-speaking world.

Carlyle was brought up in a Calvinist household by his parents, who hoped he would go into the church. However, he soon lost his faith in organised religion, instead putting his trust in work. He was also deeply affected by German Romanticism and its exploration of nature and the spiritual side of humanity. In a series of caustic essays he denounced the horrors of the Industrial Revolution – the 'Mechanical Age', as he put it. He believed that the Victorian pursuit of money and naked self-interest was corrupting human relationships. Carlyle's polemics made him an intellectual celebrity who drew such eminent Victorians as Ruskin and Browning to Cheyne Row to sit at his feet.

'Literature is the wine of life; it will not, cannot, be its food.'

Thomas Carlyle

Jane Welsh Carlyle (1801–66)

Jane Baillie Welsh was brought up in Haddington in Scotland, the only daughter of Dr John Welsh and his wife Grace. Her beloved father died in 1819 of typhus, which he had caught from a patient. Jane was bright and witty with a talent for making friends. In 1821 she was introduced to Thomas Carlyle by their mutual friend Edward Irving. Carlyle fell in love with Jane, much to the annoyance of her mother, who thought him a most unsuitable suitor for her daughter.

Married life

The Carlyles were both obsessive letter-writers – to their family, friends and to each other when apart. As a result, we probably know more about the minutiae of their domestic lives than any other Victorians.

They were a fascinating and complex couple. 'People knew the Carlyles as "literary people" of rare merit, as talented conversationalists and also quite sincere friends who were responsible for much unassuming, anonymous benevolence and charity.'

They married in 1826, and lived at Comley Bank, Edinburgh. In 1828 the Carlyles moved to Craigenputtock, a remote farm in Dumfriesshire, 'for the silence, peace and economy'. Carlyle hoped that 'I may find more health, and what I reckon weightier, more scope to improve and worthily employ myself…' But Jane was not so sure. She had resisted the idea before they married, writing to Carlyle, 'You and I keeping house at Craigenputtock! I would just as soon think of building myself a nest on the Bass Rock.'

Jane was busier than ever, in good health and spirits, but Carlyle could not settle and feared he would never be well. Jane wrote to a friend: 'The solitude is not so irksome as one might think – if we are cut off from good society, we are also delivered from bad; the roads are less pleasant to walk on than the pavements of Princes Street but we have horses to ride; and instead of shopping and making calls, I have bread to bake and chickens to hatch. I read, and work, and talk with my Husband and never weary.'

'Let no woman who values peace of soul ever dream of marrying an author.'

Jane Welsh Carlyle

Below Jane Welsh Carlyle; pencil-and-wash drawing by Samuel Laurence, 1838

Move to Chelsea

Left The front door bell
Below Carlyle outside
Cheyne Row in 1859;
ink-and-wash drawing by
H. and W. Greaves

'She made the house a little Eden
round her (so neat and graceful in
its simplicity and thrifty poverty).'

Edward Irving

Craigenputtock was beginning to get on Carlyle's nerves. He was no longer sure that he wanted to be there or that he could continue with his writing: 'I care not for poverty, little even for disgrace, nothing at all for want of renown. But the horrible feeling, is when I cease my own struggle, lose the consciousness of my own strength, and become quite worldly and wicked.' He felt lonely, and Jane's health showed no signs of improving. After much deliberating, they decided to move to London.

H & W Greaves
1859

'A right old strong roomy
 brick house.'

Thomas Carlyle

'This large and comfortable
tenement … without bugs.'

Jane Welsh Carlyle

Timeline

1795	Thomas Carlyle born in Ecclefechan, Annandale, Dumfriesshire
1801	Jane Baillie Welsh born in Haddington
1809-13	Thomas Carlyle studies at Edinburgh University
1826	Thomas Carlyle and Jane Baillie Welsh marry
1828	They move to Craigenputtock in Dumfriesshire
1833	*Sartor Resartus* published
1834	Move to 5 (now 24) Cheyne Row in London
1835	Only manuscript of the first volume of *The French Revolution* accidentally destroyed.
1837	Rewritten *French Revolution* published
1843	*Past and Present* published
1845	T*he Life and Letters of Oliver Cromwell* published
1858-65	*Frederick the Great* published
1866	Jane Welsh Carlyle dies
1881	Thomas Carlyle dies in the Drawing Room at 24 Cheyne Row
1882-4	J.A. Froude's *Life of Carlyle* published
1883	Froude's edition of Jane Welsh Carlyle's letters published
1895	Carlyle's House opened to the public
1936	Carlyle's House transferred to the National Trust

Below Cheyne Row today

On Tuesday, 10 June 1834 the Carlyles moved to 5 (now 24) Cheyne Row. Carlyle told his brother John: 'a Hackney Coach, loaded to the roof and beyond it with luggage and live-passengers, tumbled us all down here about eleven in the morning…' Jane in her enthusiasm wrote to old Mrs Carlyle: 'I could not have made myself a better house if I had had money at command… my husband will be healthier and happier than he has been for long years'. The rent was a modest £35 a year (and stayed the same for the 47 years of his tenure). This was to be the Carlyles' home for the rest of their lives.

The House

The Entrance Hall

The Entrance Hall immediately establishes the authentic mood of the house. (Only one window in the house faces south.) The Carlyles' landlord installed gas lighting in 1852, but only over the front door and in the Kitchen. The rest of the house was lit with oil lamps and candles.

The early 18th-century pine panelling was papered over in 1852 and painted to resemble stained oak.

The Parlour

This room has changed very little since Robert Tait painted the Carlyles in it in 1857. Thomas is shown wearing one of his favourite striped silk dressing gowns and holding an old-fashioned long-stemmed pipe. The armchair in which Jane is sitting is still here. Not surprisingly, the Carlyles were impatient sitters. Jane complained, 'The dog is the only member of the family who has reason to be pleased with his likeness as yet!' Jane's Maltese cross terrier Nero (pictured on the sofa on the far right) had arrived in 1849, and soon made friends

Above The floral wallpaper in the Parlour

Below The Parlour

Below left The Entrance Hall

with Thomas, who took it on long night walks through Chelsea. 'He gives it raisins, of which it is very fond, one by one, and blows tobacco smoke in its face which it does not like so much – and calls it "you little villain" in a tone of great kindness.' Nero was buried in the back garden with his own headstone (now gone).

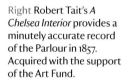

Jane ('Jenny') Welsh Carlyle welcomes their friend and neighbour, the poet Leigh Hunt, in the Parlour:

'Jenny kiss'd me when we met
Jumping from the chair she sat in; …
Say I'm weary, say I'm sad,
Say that health and wealth have missed me,
Say I'm growing old, but add,
Jenny kiss'd me.'

Piano

Jane would sit singing Scottish ballads at the piano, which came from her mother's home in 1842. She wrote to her cousin in 1848, 'But I went to hear Chopin too – once in private and once at a morning concert and Chopin has been *here!!* I never heard the piano played before – could not have believed the capabilities that lie in it.' Carlyle remembered how, a few weeks before her death, 'she turned round to her piano, got out the Thomson Burns book, and to my surprise and joy, broke out into her bright little stream of harmony'.

'Unfashionable in the highest degree, but in the highest degree comfortable and serviceable.'

Thomas Carlyle on 24 Cheyne Row

Right Robert Tait's *A Chelsea Interior* provides a minutely accurate record of the Parlour in 1857. Acquired with the support of the Art Fund.

The Back Dining Room
The China Closet
The Stairs

Left *The Back Dining Room*; watercolour painted by Helen Allingham in June 1881, shortly after Carlyle's death. It shows the scrap-screen created by Jane, which is now in the Drawing Room upstairs.

The Back Dining Room
The Carlyles chose to have their breakfast in this room as it enjoyed the best of the morning sun. They would eat Scotch porridge or bread homemade to Jane's recipe, all washed down with coffee from Fortnum & Mason.

'It is here where we sit in dewy morning sunshine, and breakfast on hot coffee and the best of bread and butter.'

Thomas Carlyle, 1834

'The old house in Cheyne Row is one of the first things I remember when we come to London. Its stillness, its dimness, its panelled walls, its carved banisters and Nero the doggie in his little coat, barking and trembling in every limb. And the enchanting screen covered with pictures, prints, and portraits without end.'

W. M. Thackeray

Furnishings

Original pieces include the small *round table* and the large mahogany sideboard. The *bird-cage* recalls that which held Jane's pet canary Chico.

The pictures include views of houses in Scotland lived in by members of the Carlyle and Welsh families.

The China Closet

The window was inserted in 1843, when the china shelves were taken down and the panelling papered over to make it part of the Back Dining Room.

'... a china room, or pantry, or I know not what, all shelved, and fit to hold crockery for the whole street.'

Thomas Carlyle, 1834

A secret delivery

The Carlyles had no children, and the young rarely entered the house. However, in 1864 their maid Mary gave birth to an illegitimate child in the China Closet. Thomas was taking tea with Geraldine Jewsbury in the next room when Mary went into labour, but she somehow managed to keep this event from him and to smuggle the baby secretly out of the house overnight.

The Stairs

Beyond the stairs is the garden door, which Carlyle kept open, as he liked fresh air. It did, however, make the house draughty.

'Broadish stair, with massive balustrade (in the old style) corniced and thick as one's thigh.'

Thomas Carlyle

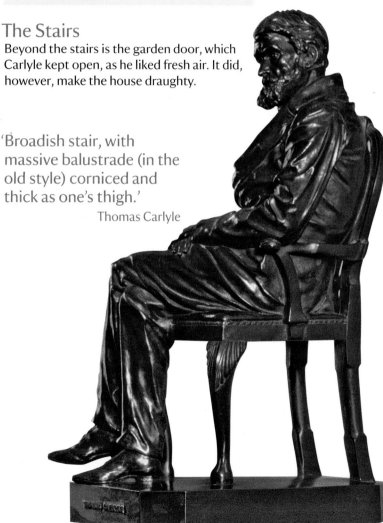

Left Dutch tiles in the fireplace

Below J.E. Boehm's statuette of Carlyle. The full-size version stands at the bottom of Cheyne Row on the Chelsea Embankment

The Drawing Room

'Home between five and six, with mud mackintoshes off, and the nightmares locked up for a while; … but first always came up for half an hour to the drawing-room and her; where a bright kindly fire was sure to be burning (candles hardly lit, all in trustful chiaroscuro) and a spoonful of brandy in water with a pipe of tobacco (which I had learned to take sitting on the rug)…. Oh, those evening half-hours, how beautiful and blessed they were.'

Thomas Carlyle

This room began life as Carlyle's library and study, where he wrote *The French Revolution*, which secured his reputation. But he found it difficult to work here because he was continually being disturbed by the neighbours' piano-playing and the traffic in the street outside.

In 1852 the room was enlarged and the windows lengthened to create a more spacious and lighter drawing room, where the Carlyles could entertain their increasingly large circle of distinguished guests. The ever-frugal Jane offered them tea and tiny sugar biscuits. Especially honoured friends and guests would be invited to stay for supper, which the Carlyles ate early.

Left **The Drawing Room**

Above Carlyle reading in the Drawing Room in 1878; watercolour by Helen Allingham

Left The scrap-screen in the Drawing Room was decorated by Jane Welsh Carlyle

Furnishings

The *scrap-screen* was created in 1849 by Jane Welsh Carlyle, who decorated it with engravings: 'I have been busy on and off, for a great many months in pasting a screen … all over with prints. It will be a charming "work of art" when finished'. It became one of Thomas's favourite memories of Jane.

The *reading chair* with its rotating book-rest was given to Carlyle by his friend John Forster on his 80th birthday. In his last months he would sit, read and doze here, and it was in this room that he died at 8.30 am on 5 February 1881.

A literary disaster

On the evening of 6 March 1835 Carlyle's friend, the philosopher John Stuart Mill, was ushered into this room, 'pale, unable to speak … the very picture of desperation'. Eventually, Mill managed to blurt out the awful news: his servant had mistakenly thrown on the fire the manuscript of the first volume of Carlyle's *French Revolution*. The only copy of Carlyle's book was '*irrevocably* ANNIHILATED'. Carlyle had no choice but to start again and rewrite the entire work from scratch. This is one of the few surviving fragments.

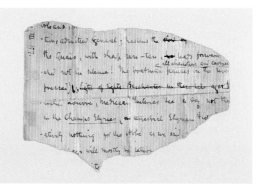

Jane's Bedroom
Jane's Dressing Room

Jane's Bedroom

Jane was a poor sleeper and tried several rooms in search of a good night's rest. She finally settled here, where she spent much of her later life, as her health worsened. As well as insomnia, she suffered from severe headaches, winter coughs and flu and neuralgia, which she tried to alleviate with large doses of morphia. Carlyle slept in the bedroom immediately above.

Her beloved dog Nero, who served as a substitute for the child she never had, was allowed to sleep on the bed.

Jane's Dressing Room

The house had no separate bathroom or lavatory. The Carlyles had to use the privy in the garden. She washed herself with a jug and basin at the marble-topped mahogany washstand, or in a hipbath with hot water carried up from the basement Kitchen by the maid. The washstand was a Christmas present from Carlyle in 1850, which came with a note: 'Blessings on her bonny face, and be it ever blithe to me, as it is dear, blithe or not.'

Above Jane's Bedroom

Opposite Jane's Dressing Room

Unwanted visitors
In 1849 Jane discovered that her favourite red bed was infested with bugs: 'All my curtains have been frantically torn down and sent to the dyers; not so much to have the colour renewed, as to have the bugs boiled to death'.

'Both husband and wife had genius; they loved each other; but what can genius and love avail against bugs and tin baths and pumps in the basement?'

Virginia Woolf

The Attic

Above Carlyle's desk in the Attic

Carlyle was hypersensitive to noise, in particular the early morning crowing of cockerels in his neighbours' back gardens and the playing of Italian organ grinders in the street outside. He finally could bear it no longer and called in the builders to make him a soundproof study in the attic. This was reached by a new staircase based on the existing pattern. Double walls were built at the front and back, and the space between them left empty to help make the room soundproof. The skylight was double-glazed with a pair of horizontally sliding sash-windows. Despite all these measures, the room was not a success. Indeed, Carlyle found to his horror that his attic refuge admitted a whole new range of noises – the whistles of railway engines and the horns of boats on the river. As Jane sadly

The writer at work

Carlyle found the process of writing agonising. Despite being disturbed by noisy neighbours, he preferred to work at home rather than in the British Museum Library. He founded the London Library (a private subscription library) so that he could borrow the reference books he needed for his work: 'To all readers the buzz and bustle of a public room is an importunate distraction; to this waste of faculty add waste of time in coming and going; waste of patience in waiting; add discomfort, perturbation, headache, waste of health ....'

reported, 'The silent room is the noisiest in the house. Mr C. is very much out of sorts.' Even so, Carlyle put up with these distractions for the next twelve years while he was writing *Frederick the Great*.

Furnishings

This is one of the least altered rooms in the house. In the centre is his writing desk. The pictures include engravings of the German historical figures who feature in *Frederick the Great*: 'In all my poor Historical investigations it has been, and always is, one of the most primary wants to procure a bodily likeness of the personage enquired after.' Not surprisingly, Carlyle campaigned for the foundation of the National Portrait Gallery in 1856.

Books

Carlyle had been a voracious book-buyer since his student days, but only a small fraction of his collection survives here. He gave the books he acquired when writing about Cromwell and Frederick the Great to Harvard University. Many were also sold by his nephew at Sotheby's in 1932, which must have included presentation copies from his eminent contemporaries such as Dickens and Tennyson. Much of what survives is not in English, notably a 31-volume edition of the works of the German writer Goethe, which was presented to Carlyle by his hero. There are also 97 volumes of Voltaire, annotated with pungent comments by Carlyle.

Right Frederick the Great was the subject of Carlyle's last great work, which was written in the Attic. Copy after T. Franke

Below The Attic

'At length, after deep deliberation, I have decided to have a top story put upon the house, one big apartment, 20 feet square, with thin *double* walls, light from the top, &c., and artfully ventilated, – into which no sound *can* come; and all the cocks in nature may crow round it, without my hearing a whisper of them!'

Thomas Carlyle, 1853

The Kitchen

Elizabeth Sprague '… is far the most loveable servant I ever had…. My only fear about her is that being only four-and-twenty, and calculated to produce an impression on the other sex, she may weary of single services'.

Jane Welsh Carlyle

The kitchen technology at Cheyne Row was primitive when the Carlyles moved in and it remained so throughout their lives. Water had to be pumped up by hand from a well under the floor. The hand pump was still in use after 1852, when mains water was laid on. A new range, made in Edinburgh, and gas lighting were put in at the same time.

Cooking

Both the Carlyles had delicate digestions, so the food cooked here had to be plain and simple: grilled mutton chops, boiled potatoes, steamed milk puddings and beef or chicken broth were among their favourites. Food attracted pests: mice and large black beetles were a particular problem, which cats were employed to reduce.

Carlyle's House, The Kitchen.

The Servant Problem

During Jane Carlyle's time, there was a single live-in servant – a maid-of-all-work who not only had to clean the house, but carry hot water up to the bedrooms, and do all the cooking. For this exhausting work, she was paid only £12 a year. In the early years, the maid had to manage without a bedroom, sleeping on a fold-up bed in the Kitchen. Carlyle would often have an evening smoke in the Kitchen, which meant that the maid was not able to go to bed until he had retired upstairs. Jane was also not the easiest of employers. Although she took on a new servant with the highest of hopes, she soon began to find fault. Angry scenes were common, followed by the sack. In her 32 years here, she got through no fewer than 34 servants. The only one to stay any length of time was Helen Mitchell from Kirkcaldy, and she eventually had to be dismissed when she was found 'mortal drunk' in 1849.

Opposite The Kitchen about 1900

Above A maid at the window in 1857

Right The Kitchen

The Carlyles' Circle

'I would go further to see Carlyle than any man alive!'

Charles Dickens

The Carlyles were encouraged to settle at Cheyne Row by the presence nearby of their friend, the poet Leigh Hunt, and although Chelsea was then far from fashionable London, they drew increasing numbers of their friends and acquaintances to the house. Despite their caustic personalities, both Thomas and Jane had a talent for friendship. Their wide literary circle included such distinguished figures as the philosopher John Stuart Mill and the novelists Dickens, George Eliot and Thackeray. Carlyle attracted disciples from across the world, and particularly in the United States, where his admirers included Ralph Waldo Emerson and Charles Eliot Norton. Although Carlyle recoiled from being lionised by Victorian society, his literary success brought fame and the consequences of celebrity. He was increasingly invited out to smart society parties, but became more reclusive after Jane's death in 1866.

'Tom Carlyle lives in perfect
dignity in a little house in Chelsea
with a snuffy Scotch maid to
open the door and the best
company in England ringing at it.'

Thackeray

'History is the essence of
innumerable biographies.'

Thomas Carlyle

Harriet, Lady Ashburton; lithograph by Frank Holl (below). Lady Ashburton was a proud aristocrat who married a member of the immensely wealthy Baring banking family. She formed one of the leading literary salons of

'God keep us all
from the madness
of popularity.'

Thomas Carlyle

the mid-19th century, which had Thomas Carlyle at its heart. He called her 'a glorious Queen', the 'lamp of my dark path'. Jane resented Lady Ashburton's influence over her husband and was less complimentary: 'She is immensely *large* – might easily have been one of the *ugliest* women living – but *is* almost beautiful – simply through the intelligence and cordiality of her expression.'

The poet *Tennyson* (below) paid a visit in September 1840. Carlyle described him as 'a fine large-featured, dim-eyed, bronze-coloured, shaggy-headed man … dusty, smoky, free-and-easy: who swims, outwardly and inwardly, with great composure in an inarticulate element as of tranquil chaos and tobacco-smoke'. This portrait by Samuel Laurence and Edward Burne-Jones was painted about the same date.

The exiled Italian patriot *Giuseppe Mazzini* (above) was befriended by the Carlyles, who helped find him lodgings in the nearby King's Road. He was a regular visitor to Cheyne Row in the 1840s. Carlyle thought him 'a most valiant, faithful, considerably gifted and noble soul; but hopelessly given up to his republicanisms'. Although, perhaps inevitably, they fell out over politics, Mazzini warmed to the Carlyles, because 'they don't have the usual insular prejudices'. He became particularly close to Jane, 'a wife of talent, of generous spirit, but sickly', but protested that he loved her only 'as a sister'.

The Garden

'Our piece of garden is all dug, and has wall-flower blossoms,
plum blossoms, vines budding, and much *spearmint*.'

Thomas Carlyle

It is a typical London garden – a narrow rectangle enclosed by high brick walls. Although the soil was poor and the planting neglected when the Carlyles moved in, Thomas was keen to grow fruit and vegetables here, and did much of the work himself, using gardening tools provided by his brother Alick. He successfully grew beans and turnips and planted new fruit trees when the old ones failed. His garden included a vine, and cherry, plum and walnut trees, rose and lilac bushes, wallflowers and mint. However, Jane's delicate digestion could not cope with raw fruit, and she had doubts about her husband's horticultural abilities: 'Mr C. does not know a myrtle from a nettle!'

The garden was one of Thomas's favourite places to relax. In the early morning or evenings he would don his broad-brimmed straw hat and dressing gown, fill a pipe and stroll solitarily up and down. In very hot weather he would bring a table and kitchen chair out into the garden and sit and write under an awning or in a shady corner. When he couldn't sleep, he would come out here and stare up at the heavens.

Within the box hedging are foxgloves, ferns, geraniums, laurel, and Virginia creepers and a pear tree.

Right Carlyle photographed in the garden by Robert Tait in 1857 **Opposite** The garden

'We have not yet ceased to admire the union of quietness, and freshness of air, and the outlook into green trees, … with the close neighbourhood of the noisiest Babylon that ever raged and *fumed* (with coal smoke) on the face of this Planet.'

Thomas Carlyle

'We found him sitting after dinner, with his pipe, in the small flagged court between the house and the garden. He was then fifty four years old; tall (about five feet eleven), thin, his body was angular, his face beardless.'

J.A. Froude on Carlyle

Creative Chelsea

'To the people of Chelsea a figure as … seemingly indestructible as Queen Victoria herself.'

J.A.M. Whistler on Carlyle

Throughout the 19th century, this corner of Chelsea attracted artists and writers because of its cheap rents, raffish atmosphere and the visual appeal of the Thames.

The potter William de Morgan lived at 8 (now 30) Cheyne Row and had his pottery at Orange House (now the site of the church of the Holy Redeemer). No.35 Glebe Place at the north end of Cheyne Row was built as a studio house in 1868–70 by the leading Arts and Crafts architect Philip Webb for the landscape painter George Price Boyce. No.49 Glebe Place is the only London building by the Scottish architect Charles Rennie Macintosh.

The novelist Mrs Gaskell was born in 1810 at 93 Cheyne Walk, and George Eliot spent her last years at no.4. Cheyne Walk was home to three great painters: J.M.W. Turner (at no.119), the Pre-Raphaelite D.G. Rossetti (at no.16), and J.A.M. Whistler (at nos.21, 96 and 119). Between 1849 and his death in 1853 the painter John Martin lived in Lindsey House on Cheyne Walk, where he completed his three largest and most famous scenes of biblical apocalypse, *The Last Judgement, The Great Day of His Wrath* and *The Plains of Heaven* (now in Tate Britain). Whistler commissioned the White House from the architect E.W. Godwin in nearby Tite Street, but, sadly, this radical building was demolished in the 1960s. Whistler was fascinated by the river people and the nocturnal moods of the

Left A William de Morgan lustreware plate

Opposite *Arrangement in Grey and Black, No.2: Thomas Carlyle*; painted by James Abbott McNeill Whistler, 1872–3

Thames. Although Carlyle and Whistler were neighbours for many years, they don't seem to have met until the early 1870s, when Whistler asked Carlyle to sit for him. The result, entitled *Arrangement in Grey and Black, No.2*, adopts the pose of Whistler's famous portrait of his mother and is one of the artist's most searching works.

'He was to me one of the real greatnesses of England.'

The painter William Holman Hunt on Carlyle

The Shrine

'It is an idle question to ask whether his books will be read a century hence. If they were all burnt on his funeral pile, it would only be like cutting down an oak after its acorns have sown a forest. For there is hardly a superior or active mind of his generation that has not been modified by Carlyle's writings.'

George Eliot

The peace of Carlyle's final days was interrupted by reporters repeatedly ringing the front door bell, eager to get the news of his death, but he was too ill to register this last disturbance.

The publication in 1882–4 of J.A. Froude's four-volume life of Carlyle and his edition of Jane's letters revealed the true nature of the Carlyles' marriage and provoked one of the great Victorian literary rows. But the controversy soon subsided, as Carlyle's rhetorical prose style and political views went out of fashion.

A commemorative plaque was placed on the front of the house, but when George Lumsden, a Manchester businessman and Carlyle devotee, paid a visit to Cheyne Row in 1894, he was alarmed to find that the house had become a dingy refuge for stray cats and dogs. Despite little public enthusiasm, he decided to launch a campaign to buy the house and open it to visitors. The Carlyle's House Purchase Fund (chaired by Virginia Woolf's father, Leslie Stephen) succeeded in acquiring the freehold in May 1895, and the Carlyle House Memorial Trust was set up to run it. The house was opened in July that year, with much of its original contents returned on loan or presented to the Trust.

Between 1895 and 1917 the custodian was Mrs Isabella Strong, who showed Virginia Woolf round in 1909. Carlyle's House continued to be shown in this quiet way until 1936, when ownership was transferred to the National Trust, which has cherished the unique spirit of this joint literary shrine ever since.

Left Thomas Carlyle; albumen photograph by Julia Margaret Cameron, 1867. Carlyle commented, 'It is as if suddenly the picture began to speak, terrifically ugly and woe-begone, but has something of a likeness – my candid opinion.'

'London, happily, is becoming full of great men's houses, bought for the nation and preserved entire with the chairs they sat on and the cups they drank from, their umbrellas and their chests of drawers.'

Virginia Woolf, 1932